The Other Side of Broken

As Told to Henrietta Brown

Cheri Taylor

The Other Side of Broken: As Told to Henrietta Brown

© 2013 by Cheri Taylor and Cheri Taylor Ministries
Revised and reprinted March 2022. All Rights Reserved.

No part of this book may be reproduced or transmitted in any form or by any means, electronic or mechanical, including photocopying and recording, or by any information storage or retrieval sys-tem, except as may be expressly permitted in writing by the publisher. Requests for permission should be addressed in writing via email to Lily of the Valley Publishing, Inc. Requests may be sent to: publishing@mylilyofthevalley.org.

ISBN: 978-0-578-33212-3

Copyright Disclaimer under Section 107 of the Copyright Act (1976): Allowance is made for fair use for purposes such as criticism, comment, news reporting, teaching, and research. Fair use is a use permitted by copyright statute that might otherwise be infringing. Non-profit, e ducational, o r p ersonal u se t ips t he b alance in favor of fair use. Cheri Taylor Ministries is recognized by the IRS as a 501(c)3 nonprofit organization and is solely dedicated to Christian ministry.

Scripture quotations marked (KJV) are taken from the *Holy Bible, King James Version*, Cambridge, 1769 which is public domain. All rights reserved.

Scripture quotations marked (NIV) are taken from the *Holy Bible, New International Version©, NIV©*. Copyright © 1973, 1978, 1984 by Biblica, Inc. All rights reserved. www.zondervan.com

Scripture quotations marked (NKJV) taken from the New King James Version. Copyright © 1982 by Thomas Nelson, Inc. All rights reserved.

This book is designed to provide accurate and authoritative information with regard to the subject matter covered. This information is given with the understanding that neither the author nor Lily of the Valley Publishing, Inc. is engaged in rendering legal, professional advice. Since the details of your situation are face dependent, you should additionally seek the services of a competent professional.

Published by Lily of the Valley Publishing, Inc.
Santa Claus, Indiana 47579 USA | 812.661.1323 | www.mylilyofthevalley.org | publishing@mylilyofthevalley.org

Cover design by Tammy Sumner | Sumwhatsouth's Digital Palette - www.sumwhatsouth.com
Content editing and interior design by Kevin Miller: https://www.book-editing.com/kevin-miller/
Author photo by Rhonda Hunter, Style Photography

Contents

Acknowledgements	7
Foreword	11
Preface	13
Thoughts from a Friend	17
1 - Background & Calling	25
2 - Mr. Drummer	35
3 - Broken Reality	43
4 - Emotional War	51
5 - Jeff's Story	61
6 - Learning from the Eagles	73
7 - Rebuilding His Temple	81
8 - Restoration Through Repentance	89
9 - God's Strength Is Sufficient	93
10 - His Healing Power	101
On the Other Side	107
Notes	113
About the Author	115

Acknowledgements

When I think of those who have helped me through this journey, many names and faces come to mind. These are some of the special ones.

My Lord and Savior, Jesus Christ: You have always been and will continue to be my true source of healing and inspiration. You're the only reason I have been able to stay on the path to wholeness. A simple thank-you will never be enough. I pray that my life will always be a testimony of Your greatness. I look forward with anticipation to the day I will see You face to face and bow at Your feet.

Greg: You are my true white knight. I know that I could not fulfill this call on my life to the fullest without your love and support. I love you more than words can ever express.

Heather: Through all my hurt and sorrow, I also cried for you. Coming from a broken home is difficult to overcome. You were the light in my dark world, and today you still bring me such joy. God has been good to us. I'm so proud of the beautiful woman, wife, and mother that you've become.

Philip: Never in my wildest dreams did I think I would be the mother of a United States Marine. Talk about an emotional rollercoaster! I'm so proud of the man, husband, and father you've become. However, I also know that there's music inside of your very being that desires to play aloud. Do it for Him, my son, and you will be blessed!

Charles and Johnlyn Criss (a.k.a. Dad and Mom): I'm so thankful that the Lord allowed me to be called your daughter. You have given me nothing but unconditional love and support. Thank you for showing me the way to Jesus through your words and actions.

Naomi: My sweet mother-in-love, you are the best. You have faced so many trials and heartaches throughout your life, and yet your smile always shines. Thank you and Lee for accepting Heather and me into your family and loving us as if we've always been part of it.

Henrietta: Many years ago, the Lord placed the desire in my heart to tell this story, but I didn't know how. I have been so amazed by how He has placed different people in my life to help me fulfill His calling. The gifts of writing, teaching, and wise counsel that you have been given mean more to me than I can ever express with mere words. Thank you, my friend.

The Taylor Family

Charles & Johnlyn Criss

Foreword

It's an old, old story. The difference is that Cheri, through the changeless Word of God, godly friends, and a determination to know God's will for her life, has a story with a joyous ending. Cheri tells her story to help you see that God's love is a constant in all of our lives. A song on one of her earlier projects boldly proclaims, "No One Loves Me Like You (Jesus)."

My friendship with Cheri Taylor has been forged in the gospel. As I have observed her minister here at home, in Jamaica, and in Romania, she proclaims a wonderful saving and healing message.

She is authentic; she truly walks in the Spirit. The words in this book will help you if you are hurting and also help you as you help others who are hurting.

"Blessed be God, even the Father of our Lord Jesus Christ, the Father of mercies, and the God of all comfort; Who comforters us in all our tribulation, that we may be able to comfort them which are in any trouble, by the comfort wherewith we ourselves are comforted of God" (2 Cor. 1:3–4, KJV).

Price Harris,
Price Harris Evangelical Association
Shreveport, LA

Preface

A few years ago, I clearly heard the Lord say, "Write it down."

"But Lord," I protested, "I'm not a writer!"

Again, He said, "Write it down. Let them know all that I've brought you through and how I continue to heal you."

Come share my journey to *The Other Side of Broken*. Let me show you how I left behind the heartache and tears, experiencing the miracle of restoration firsthand. The comfort and peace that Jesus placed within me is still at work today as He has called me to share the gospel with all who will listen. My goal is not to change anyone's theology about divorce. I simply want to tell you what Jesus did for me.

> The gifts and callings of God are irrevocable. (Rom. 11:29, KJV)

These words ring through my head as I begin to share my story with you. God, who is omniscient (all-knowing), was aware that I would become a Christian at a young age. He knew He would call me to a specific task, but because God (from the beginning of creation) gives each of us the gift of free will, He also knew that I would not always do exactly as I should.

To put it in today's terms, "stuff happens," and we have to deal with it. However, from a Christian standpoint, we don't have to deal with it alone. We have Divine help, and that's what makes the difference. This story is about the "stuff" that happened and what God has done to allow the broken pieces of my life to be used for Him.

> Right here,
> on the other side of broken
> Where my heart has found
> a refuge in the Lord
> Right here,
> where the door
> is always open
> And His healing
> is mine to receive
> Right here,
> on the other side of broken
> I can be free.

From "The Other Side of Broken"

by Amy Morris

Thoughts from a Friend

Everyone encounters brokenness at one stage or another. If we look at the Hebrew words that are translated as "broken-hearted," we find it literally means "shattered soul." Our soul or heart is what we think, what we desire, and what we feel—our mind, will and emotions. One only needs to read the Psalms to understand this.

Jesus was sent to heal the broken-hearted. As Jesus says in Luke 4:18, "The Spirit of the Lord *is* upon me, because He hath anointed me to preach the gospel to the poor; He hath sent me to heal the broken-hearted."

Earlier in the Bible, God rebukes the pastors/shepherds of Israel because they did not bring people to a healing of their hearts (Ez. 34:16). We are in the same position today where many people are broken, but some are turning these people away like lepers who cannot be fixed. Why are relational break-downs like divorce such a leprous disease in the eyes of today's churches? Anyone who has gone through a divorce is broken. They have experienced trauma that has wounded their soul. However, some cast such people out, saying that God can't use them. Well, maybe in their broken state He can't, but He restoreth my soul (Ps. 23)! David knew he was broken, but David also knew that God was his healer, and he reached out to Him, as recounted in Psalm 77:6 (KJV): "I call to remembrance my song in the night: I commune with mine own heart: and my spirit made diligent search."

to be validated. We need to know that it is OK to be angry and to feel hurt or rejected. When we realize that everything we feel is real and acceptable, it helps us understand that we are not crazy or wrong to feel such emotions. When we read the Psalms, we see how David went through this process. This will blow your mind; David ventilated unto the Lord. All Scripture is inspired by God, which means David's ventilations are from God! It's OK to ventilate to God. He will hear, and He will validate.

4. Vindication – This is a fancy word for forgiveness. We can't get to the forgiveness stage before ventilation and validation. Good people in their right minds do not hurt others. So, when they do hurt others, clearly they are under the influence of something else, such as substances, false beliefs, or even something demonic. (Even Peter was even in-

fluenced by the devil, so none of us are immune.) Often, people hurt others because they have been hurt themselves and have not healed from that. Thus, hurting others seems to be a way for them to feel better. In light of this, forgiveness is not letting the other person win but simply saying, "I do not want to do to you what you have done to me." In this process, we win! To stop our own hurt, we need to stop them and their actions living on in our minds.

5. eViction – I realize this isn't a real V, but this is where we need to get rid of the thoughts, lies, and wicked ideas that have kept us down for so long. Cast them out in the name of Jesus, and walk away in freedom.

No matter how you've been broken, Jesus can and will heal you if you are willing to commune with your own heart

Ephesians 5:19 (KJV) encourages us to follow David's example: "Speaking to yourselves in psalms and hymns and spir-itual songs, singing and making melody in your heart to the Lord."

Scripture tells us to speak with our hearts, especially the broken parts, and let the LORD shine His light in and heal those wounds. Paul tells the church at Colossae that they should practice this with one another also (Col. 3:16). When did we reach the point where we can restore a brother or sister who has been an adulterer but not restore a divorcee?

Furthermore, will God call and use someone who is living in sin? No! So, the fact that God *is* calling and using divorced people is proof that we have a gross misunderstanding of scripture. Under Hebrew law, a separation *and* a bill of divorcement would annul the marriage and, thus, free people from the union. If one was only separated, they would still be married and would be committing adultery if they married another. This is what Jesus was talking about. If you don't believe this, I ask you once again, would God call and use someone who was living in sin?

I have counseled many divorced people who have been shunned, guilted, and rebuked by friends, family, and church members who have made them feel useless in God's eyes. These are the lies of the devil that many Christians are happy to spread! After counseling divorcees and bringing them through our program of the "5 Vs," God is using them mightily in many ways!

Let me share the 5 Vs with you.

1. Violation – Our souls are violated by abuse, trauma, or whatever caused us to break.
2. Ventilation – Those who have been violated need to talk with a trusted counselor, friend, or simply with the Lord.
3. Validation – Our emotions need

and with God. Let the Lord bring up, deal with, and heal your pain, so He can re-store your soul once again!

Pastor Dr. Bob Strachan
Jedburg Baptist Church - Scotland

1
Background & Calling

Every Sunday morning, Sunday night, and Wednesday night, we were there, in church. Growing up in a Christian home, it didn't matter if we were in revival, a special service, a business meeting, a marriage, funeral, or fellowship gathering, when the church doors were open, the Criss family was there.

Daddy was a deacon, Sunday School teacher, song leader, and a member of the local Gideon camp, all while working on various committees throughout the years. Mom taught Sunday School and Vacation Bible School, filled in during the absence of the regular piano player, and hauled carloads of people to and from church. Our home was always open for meals with the pastor's family, various youth gatherings, and traveling evangelists or missionaries who came through on occasion. They didn't do anything of this because they felt obligated or thought it was the right thing to do; they did it because they loved Jesus and simply wanted to share His blessings with others.

While my parents worked to support our small family and busy church life, their main goal was teaching my sister and me about the Lord's love for us. The foundations of the faith were taught through the songs of old like "Amazing Grace," "It Is Well with My Soul," "How Firm a Foundation," and many others. Missing Sunday School to get an extra hour of sleep was never an option. Bible drills, Bible study, youth group, and choir practice were normal parts of life. From the day I was born (and even now), our lives revolved around our church.

One evening a few days before my tenth birthday, the Holy Spirit spoke to me during a revival service. It wasn't an audible voice but a sweet wooing that opened my eyes to the fact that I needed a Savior. I knew that I could not make it to heaven on my mom and dad's coattails. I also understood that I needed my own relationship with Jesus. That evening, I went to the altar, confessed my sins, and asked Jesus to be my Savior. From that moment on, I have been confident in the salvation that He has given me. Even during the lowest points of my life, I still knew that God alone was my hope, my joy, my all. Everything I know, everything I have, and everything I am comes from Jesus, my source. I know I'm saved!

Today, it's still typical for me to walk into my parents' home and find one or both of them with their Bible in hand reading scripture and spending time at our Savior's feet. I still have vivid memories of my dad on his knees, quietly calling out to his Lord as he used the couch for his altar. How comforting it is to know that many of those prayers were, and still are, for me.

As I ponder these precious memories, I'm reminded that my parents didn't just tell me how to live a life pleasing to the Lord; they lived it by example! Spending time in the Word and prayer are two essential parts of my life. I'm so thankful for the example they set for me.

Submitting to God's will hasn't always been easy, but I've always known that if I was going to find success that brought Him glory, it was a necessary thing to do. In Romans 12:1–2, Paul says we need to present ourselves to God in a sacrificial manner because this is a reasonable thing to do. He goes on to say that instead of aligning our minds with the world, we need to allow our minds to be renewed to line up with God's will. For the most part, from the moment I understood this,

I've put myself in His hands and let Him be in charge of my life. He's not just God to me; He's my Lord and best Friend. Believe me when I say that I have failed Him miserably many times and tried doing things on my own, but I can also say that, from where I am now in my life, I have discovered that God's way is always the best way.

Not long after I was born again, I began to sense God's call on my life for His service, but because of my young age, I didn't fully understand the meaning of that calling. However, I wanted to be obedient. After sharing this with my pastor, all I could do was continue to grow in my life as a follower of Christ. Even as a child and into my early teen years, I became increasingly sensitive to His leading. Many times I heard Him whisper, "I have something special for you to do." It was never audible, but I heard Him, nevertheless.

The thought of being used by God was exciting to me. I started to think of people I knew at church and watched to see what they did. Our pastor was a man, and all of the other churches I knew had male pastors. This led me to conclude that God was not calling me to be a pastor. My reasoning may have been flawed, but it turns out that my conclusion was correct. Continuing to pay attention to the ministry of others, I realized that some Sunday School teachers were women, but teaching was not what they did as a profession; they were volunteers. When God said, "something special," I assumed it would involve what I would do for a living. Again, because of my age, I didn't understand that teaching Sunday school or Bible study was a calling!

The only women I knew who made their living in a "Christian" occupation were missionaries, so in my young mind, I decided that had to be the "something special" God wanted me to do. In retrospect, that conclusion wasn't too far off the mark.

As time moved on and I grew into my middle teens, my sense of calling became somewhat buried by other things in life. My mother, however, was a different story.

I told her about my thoughts and feelings about God's call on me and, like Mary, the mother of Jesus, she kept these things and "pondered them in her heart." I had begun singing as a small child, and the older I got, the deeper my passion became. I still didn't understand that this would be wrapped up in the call that God had placed on my life. When I entered my teen years (along with all the things that involves) sometimes I would picture myself standing before crowds of people singing and speaking! In my immaturity, I thought it was just something I wanted to do for recognition and fun. I still had no idea that one could be called to sing. Like most teenagers, I identified with singers I heard on the radio or saw on television. I would look at them with stars in my eyes and daydream of what I saw as a glamorous way to live.

Cheri with *The Proclaimers*, 1983

Cheri with *His Witness*, 1989

Cheri with *His Witness*

2
Mr. Drummer

Being a Christian doesn't make us perfect; we don't always get things right. When we see something we want, we often let our desires take the place of God's will for our lives. That was the case when I met a young man who was a drummer in a local gospel group. Although I was only fifteen and not allowed to date, my parents would let me go to concerts with him, as he drummed, and the gospel group served in churches close by. When

I was seventeen and dating him, the baritone of the group resigned. I tried out as a vocalist and, surprisingly, was chosen for the position! Less than two months after my eighteenth birthday, we became "Mr. and Mrs. Drummer."

That was my plan, not God's. I'm so thankful that when any of God's children decide to go their own way, God still demonstrates His love for us in so many ways. Just as we love and care for our own children when they are disobedient, God, who is love made perfect, never does anything that is not for the good of His children. Romans 8:28 emphatically says that all things—not a few things or most things—work together for good for those who love Him and are called according to His purpose. Even in our failures, when we repent for not listening to God, He can use the grief and pain that we've caused to bring Himself glory. God is faithful, but His plan is not always obvious. When we act on our own outside His will, it can take longer for us to see the good.

I still remember the day I married Mr. "Drummer." As I prepared to walk down the aisle of the church and saw him waiting for me at the altar, I knew I was doing the wrong thing. In my heart I could hear that "still, small voice" telling me to stop, saying, "This is wrong and will not last!" Unfortunately, with all the preparations we had made and all our friends and family there, I couldn't find the courage to say no.

From day one of our marriage, I fervently tried to make it work. My husband also promised, "I'll take you places you've never been before," and that he did. The journey was rough and hard. He took me through heartache, sorrow, infidelity, mental abuse, and anguish.

Looking back, however, I can clearly see some of the good that came from that time. I can see how God carried me through every single day. I also see His hand of provision and how He taught me that He is, and always will be, everything I need.

The main blessing that came from this

union was our daughter, Heather Lyn, born just before our second anniversary.

There were times when we had no money to buy milk, but the Lord never let us down. In His perfect love, He always made a way for us to provide for our daughter. Motherhood at the age of twenty, while challenging, was a wonderful time for me.

Even though I was singing in a gospel group and married with a child, I was not conscious of the fact that the Lord was preparing me for the calling that He had placed on my life, a calling that was irrevocable. Slowly, week by week, the Lord began to show me that I was truly ministering to people through music and that this was exactly what He had called me to do.

When God places a call on someone's life, it doesn't always mean they're ready to go at that moment. Preparation through growth, study, and practice while wrapping it all up in prayer is key! If I wanted to run a marathon, there's no way I could simply walk up to the starting line and expect to run more than twenty-six miles. First, I would need to study the sport, get the proper exercise, and begin with short runs. Eating the right foods to support muscle strength, getting rid of unhealthy habits, and wearing the right kind of shoes would all be necessary components to help me prepare for the race ahead.

To minister in my calling, I had to learn and grow. Singing a song correctly and with emotion doesn't just "happen." I would often listen to a recording over and over and then practice until I had memorized it. This discipline still applies today. Then I had to consume the right kind of food—God's Word (1 Pet. 2:2). I needed to pray for the wisdom to discern His will (Jam. 1:5), and I had to lay aside the things that weighed me down (Heb. 12:1).

To accomplish all of this, I found myself spending more and more time in the Word, not just reading but seriously studying. How could I rightly pour myself into another person's life through ministry without the proper food and drink of His Word?

God's will and God's calling are two separate things. God's will determines who we are. God's calling determines what we do. God's will is that everyone should come to repentance and yield themselves completely to Him. Our thinking ought to line up with God's thinking. God's calling is the way we relate to others to glorify Him. I strive to do both with excellence, but, of course, I often fail. I'm so thankful for God's grace.

As my awareness of ministry grew, I found myself seeking out mentors who would guide me—not just teachers and preachers but also singers. I would watch how they dressed, how they sang, and how they stood on the platform. I would even take note of how they moved and held a mic!

Over the years, through God's faithfulness I have been blessed to have men and women who not only "talk the talk" but "walk the walk" come along beside me. I can trust them to speak encouragement as well as correction, with love, into my life.

Even now as I continue to grow in the Lord, I still find it necessary to have someone close by to keep me accountable. I'm not willing to run the risk of having anything in my life that may hinder my walk with the Lord. Plus, I would never want anything in my walk to cause someone else to stumble! I'm well aware of the fact that others are watching me just as I have watched others. I'm so thankful for my husband, a close friend, and my pastor, all of whom I trust to keep me in check. Most importantly, the Holy Spirit is always there guiding me. Once again, I don't always get it right, but because this is a relationship, when I do stumble, God is there to convict, forgive, and correct me.

When we have trained and prepared ourselves to answer our calling, we should never take our standing in Christ for granted. We must remember that putting on the armor of God is a daily task (Eph. 6:11–18). Oftentimes, we think we're safe because we're involved in the church, working in the center of God's will, and doing everything we think is right. But if we're not careful, we can let our defenses down. We forget the enemy is walking around like a lion, looking for someone to eat. When we forget to depend on God and start depending on ourselves and our own goodness, we become the perfect target for dinner. Christians can also follow God from the wrong place. I think we've all had times in our lives when we've either run ahead of God or fallen behind. Only when we are walking with Him side by side can the Lord make our calling clear to us.

Cheri with her dear friends, Les Butler, owner of Butler | Family Music Group and her producer for 20 years, and Mrs. Henrietta Brown

3
Broken Reality

After nearly twelve years of trying to convince myself that Mr. Drummer was my knight in shining armor, I began to notice that his armor wasn't so shiny anymore. A large area of tarnish, rust, and dirt was beginning to be more and more apparent every day. Three years of courtship and nearly nine years of marriage had really taken the blinders—and stars—from my eyes and heart. At the ripe old age of twenty-six, I found myself alone with a six-year-old child and nowhere to go except back home to Mom and Dad. Spiritually and mentally, I was so broken, battered, and bruised to the point that I didn't know if I would survive.

In my mind, my marriage was not the only thing that was over. I felt I had reached the bottom in every way—spiritually, emotionally, and physically. I had failed as a wife; I had also failed my daughter, my parents, my Lord, and myself. I thought that no one, not even God, could ever love me, want me, or have any use for me. I was an absolute and totally unredeemable mess—or so I believed. Any thoughts of being useful in God's service were buried underneath the fallout from my failure. The enemy was having a field day with my heart, soul, and mind. He convinced me that anything I had ever done, was doing, or would do would never be of any lasting value.

When we hit bottom, Satan can easily make us believe that we have not only failed but that it is our fault. I wanted my marriage to work, but I believed everything that went wrong was my fault, and Mr. Drummer did nothing to help me believe otherwise. Pleading with God to help me be a better wife was my constant prayer. I did everything I could to be all that my husband wanted and needed, but it was never enough. Finally, I had to admit that my efforts had been—and would always be—in vain.

Not only did I believe I was a failure, I also convinced myself that I was alone. I had my daughter and my parents, but that was of little comfort to me. I had no marketable skills, no money, and no foreseeable way of supporting my daughter and me. Satan had blinded me to the point that I could not see the blessings all around me.

I remember feeling unlovable, stupid, fat (I weighed about 110 pounds), ugly, and worthless. I also felt angry, humiliated, and embarrassed. God was there, and His arms were still open, but I felt like I was wrapped in a cocoon of misery. I was in such a state of grief that I couldn't see or hear Him.

The Bible is clear that God hates divorce (Mal. 2:16). At the same time, I failed to separate the fact that although the Lord hates divorce, He still loved me! Because of this, the enemy caused me to believe I was no longer usable and that I could no longer represent a holy God.

Divorce is always a painful thing. When two people become one flesh (Gen. 2:23–24), if they get divorced, it's like tearing flesh from flesh. It seems as if no amount of pressure applied to the wound can stop the bleeding. I vividly remember saying to my father, "I just want the pain to go away!" I also remember the look of sadness on his face, knowing there was nothing he could do. Looking back, all I can say is, "But God . . ."

If you would allow me some leeway, may I take a moment to compare divorce and death? In some ways they are very much the same. Divorce involves the death of our dreams and plans. It signals the end of our life, as we know it at the time. Could it then be said that, in some cases, divorce may actually be worse than the death of a spouse? When a spouse dies, it's final, and it's usually no one's fault. There is no blame to place on a person, although at the time, we may blame God. There is no asking, "What did I do wrong?" We know that the spouse who died did not leave us because of something we may or may not have said or done. Divorce, by contrast, encompasses all of these things.

In Jeremiah 18, the prophet tells us that God told him to go down to the potter's house. There God said, to Jeremiah, "I will cause you to hear my words." So, Jeremiah did as the Lord commanded and watched as the potter made a vessel on the wheel. The vessel was marred, so the potter remade it into another vessel that he liked better. Again, God spoke to Jeremiah: "Cannot I do with you as this potter?" Never forget that God will not allow us to be broken beyond repair. Just as the potter changed his vessel from one with flaws and imperfections into one that was good, God can reshape us into vessels fit for His use. Like the clay in the potter's hands, we can be assured that God doesn't throw the clay away; He uses it to remake us.

I was that marred and broken vessel. Looking back, I can now see where the gentle hand of the heavenly Potter put me on His wheel to make me new and stronger. Even today He's still working on some of the rough edges. Because He loves and wants to use me, sometimes He puts me back on that wheel. He will continue to do so until He calls me home; and even though it can be a painful process, I'm thankful.

The road to restoration was not an easy one. Besides the failure and loneliness, I had to deal with other things that I never realized were there. One of the most painful things I dealt with was the realization that I had married my "knight" outside of God's will.

Looking back at the beginning of our relationship, I see my own willfulness and desire to please myself. At that point, I wanted my glory—not God's—to be shown. So, He allowed me to go off on my own way where my knight, indeed, "took me places I'd never been before."

Only my Heavenly Father knew that my brokenness would someday become a ministry to help others. "For I know the plans I have for you, declares the Lord, plans to prosper you and not to harm you, plans to give you hope and a future. Then you will call on me and come and pray to me, and I will listen to you. You will seek me and find me when you seek me with all your heart" (Jer. 29: 11–13, NIV).

4
Emotional War

When the previous chapter's "broken reality" became my only reality, the emotional war ensued.

My anger was directed toward my circumstances. I was angry because I didn't believe that God could/would use me. I was angry with Mr. Drummer. Even though I didn't recognize it until later, I was angry because no one recognized or reaffirmed my calling. Actually, no one, with the exception of my parents, seemed to recognize that I even had a calling. It was just something I did.

As the years progressed, I didn't realize how much the chains of anger were keeping me bound. However, life marched on, and some of the more hurtful memories faded into the background. We're often told that time heals all wounds, but that's not always true. If the powerful force of anger is not dealt with, then, like an untreated cancer, it will fester and quietly destroy us from the inside out. That was the case with me.

Through the months and years after the divorce, I would often see people whom I knew during my marriage to Mr. Drummer. I found it odd that sometimes they would avoid me, and at other times they would go out of their way to talk to me, especially if they had heard some sort of juicy gossip and thought I needed to know it!

One day I reached my boiling point. I was a basket case, and I needed to talk with someone. I called my pastor, who had known me since I was a small child.

When he answered the phone, I blurted out, "Do you make house calls?"

When he arrived, the same old stuff began spewing from my heart and off my tongue. Through my bitter tears, I said, "I know this anger is going to destroy me, and I don't know how to get rid of it!" This godly man told me that it was OK to be angry. Ephesians 4:26a (NKJV) says "Be angry and sin not." He told me that sin can get in the way of how we handle anger. Retaliation is not the correct response. Then, in that sweet, still, small voice, the Lord spoke into my heart, telling me that if I was going to be all that He wanted me to be, I had to forgive and let things go. Can you imagine how it would be if God said He forgave us but then held onto His anger the way we do many times when we've been wronged? Once again, I'm so thankful for God's grace!

Praise the Lord, 1 John 1:9 (KJV) tells us, "If we confess our sins, He is faithful and just to forgive us our sins and to cleanse us from all unrighteousness."

Folks, that is freedom! It's also the only way to the "other side of broken."

My scars, both physical and emotional, remind me of injuries that have healed. The scars on my body and my heart remind me of the places where the pain has been removed.

Tearing flesh from flesh causes a deep and terrible wound. As such wounds heal, they scar. Scarred flesh is thicker, harder, and less supple than normal flesh. Things are similar when our lives are torn apart. When we experience the wounding and brokenness within, we must make sure to not allow the wound, as it heals, to cause a thickening or hardening of our spiritual eyes and ears. If we allow the hardening to continue, we will find that our wounds wrap around our hearts as well. When this happens, we become easy prey for the enemy's lies.

The enemy is so subtle in his attacks. I could hear him whisper in my ear, "You're an ugly loser, and you'll never amount to anything!" He not only uses whispers, he also uses people to do his bidding. That's when I need to remember that Jesus, who loved me so much, died on a cross and paid for my healing! Dear reader, He loves you that much, too.

From time to time, my mother has said that she can still see some of the scars that have been left. Whether that's good or bad, I don't know. However, I believe one thing my mother sees is my ongoing struggle with feelings of inferiority and insecurity. While I have confidence in my calling and God's sustaining grace, I still struggle with my ability to be all that God wants me to be.

Meeting and talking with people have never been a problem for me because most people will never know me well enough to see beneath the surface of the scars. I know many of my feelings of inadequacy stem from my first marriage and being told that I was not good enough. As Mr. Drummer told me this, he followed up by looking for someone who, I supposed, he thought was good enough.

Even today, sometimes when problems arise, my first thought is, 'Oh, it's my fault.' I always feel like I need to do more or something else so I can be "good enough." I continue to deal with this, though I have full assurance that, one day, this too will be healed.

My rejection was another ever-present gift from the enemy. He persuaded me to believe that no one but my daughter and my parents wanted me, and that God could never use me! Even though the enemy almost convinced me that I was good for nothing, in the midst of all the broken pieces, my beautiful daughter, Heather, was and continues to be a true delight in my life. Despite all the rejection, when I looked into her eyes, I felt like I could do anything! I'm so proud of the beautiful, strong, and compassionate woman she has become. She has had her own struggles in life, but that is another story for another time.

An unseen wall of rejection also grew between me and some of my friends and acquaintances. Divorce changes how some people look at you and respond to you — especially those of us in the Church who find ourselves in this situation. Where we were once part of a couple, we're now single. To avoid saying the wrong thing or having to take time to listen to us share their hearts, they simply avoid us. This is not always the case, but it happens more times than not. It's a sad commentary on how we look at others through our own eyes and not those of our compassionate Lord.

This is something that I have had to learn in my own experience of ministering to those who have gone through a divorce or another source of pain. Many times, the Holy Spirit has convicted me of when I ignored someone because I didn't want to deal with having to say the right thing or spend time listening. I'm so thankful He takes me to task, reminding me of how much it meant to have someone listen when I was in a similar situation. With His help, I try to be more sensitive to the Holy

Spirit's leading when He prompts me to stop and simply make the time.

We don't always have to know the right words to say, but quoting Scripture or reciting clichés is not always necessary. Being sensitive to the Holy Spirit's leading will tell you when to speak and when to simply listen.

I did have a wonderful friend during this time who was ready to listen anytime I needed her. I'm sure there were times she cringed when her phone rang or when she looked out the window and saw my car pulling into her driveway. But to this day, I am forever thankful to the Lord for bringing her into my life. He used her in a mighty way on my path to healing and restoration. Thank you, Deena. I will forever be grateful.

My humiliation and embarrassment were daily companions because of who and what I claimed to be. I didn't want to face anyone—my parents, friends, neighbors, or people at my parents' church. On Sunday I'd slip into the back pew as church began and then exit as soon as the pastor said, "Amen." I was so ashamed of what had happened and who I thought people perceived me to be. Yes, the enemy's lies were working well in me.

My emotional war, at the time, was crippling, painful, and devastating. At that stage of my life, I had yet to learn that God's gifts and calling are irrevocable.

5
Jeff's Story

While in a broken season or dealing with traumatic experiences, we often feel isolated. Thoughts that no one cares or understands the pain we're dealing with can be overwhelming. Also, as I stated before, sometimes those who we thought were trusted friends turn their backs on us.

With his permission, I'd like to share the story of a dear friend of mine. When he read the first printing of this book, he had yet to share with me his testimony of brokenness as a result of a divorce. However, as he read the account of my pain, grief, rejection, and lies from the enemy, his first thoughts were that I was writing about him! "How on earth did she know?"

Other people have gone through many trials and hurts that I will never be able to comprehend, never mind the raw emotions and pain that are associated with them, because I haven't experienced them. But this is one story that I can identify with. Despite the pain he experienced, I, along with Jeff, can also assure you, there is hope and healing!

Jeff's Narrative

As a pastor for over thirty years, I've been called upon by many individuals, couples, and families who have gone through or are going through an event in their life that is causing them great pain. Some of these folks have reached the point of being completely broken, both emotionally and spiritually. These folks are looking for answers, for a way to rid their lives of pain and heal their brokenness.

Many have shared with me how hopeless and alone they feel. I have to admit, sometimes I've been at a loss in terms of words of comfort and encouragement or ways to help. I have also felt helpless in trying to aid in their time of need because their pain was so deep. Their hurt was beyond anything I had ever experienced. I didn't understand what it meant or felt like to be broken. Little did I realize that was about to change.

My journey to brokenness began many years ago. Married for thirty-three years, my wife and I were blessed with two daughters and three grandchildren. But truthfully, our marriage had been over for years. I had contemplated a divorce more times than I can remember. We were both miserable. I stayed in the marriage for our daughters' sake and to keep up appearances for the ministry

By all accounts, my ministry was very

successful, but there came a time when my personal life took its toll on me and the ministry. I simply didn't care anymore. With both of our daughters grown and out of the house, the thought of going home at the end of the day made me sick. To sit down and work on a Sunday message became almost impossible. I had nothing left to give anyone! I was emotionally drained and spiritually bankrupt. After thirty-three years of marriage, I filed for divorce, resigned from my church, and left the ministry.

Our divorce was far more painful than I ever dreamed it would be. On many levels I felt like a total failure as a husband, father, grandfather, and as a pastor. I had reconciled in my mind that in the near future, I would be OK. I wasn't the only person who had ever gone through a divorce. I knew many divorced people who seemed just fine. However, the problem I was facing was something that I never saw coming.

Over all those years in ministry, I had met and became friends with other pastors and church leaders from all over the United States and Poland. They prayed for me and my ministry, called me their friend, and told me they loved and cared about me. But when I began my journey through a dark time in my life, they forgot they ever knew me. They never called to check on me, tell me they were praying for me, or visited me. To this day, most of them still don't speak to me. I found out the hard way that I was only useful to many and loved by many if I could help them in some way in their time of need.

So many others in the Christian community, just like all those pastors and church leaders, turned their backs on me. They gossiped and spread rumors about the life they thought I was leading. Never once did they want to know the truth. I was told by many that God would never use me again. I was nothing and a nobody. Finally, I knew what it was like to be totally broken, alone, and bitter. The one place in this world—the Church—that I thought I could turn to for rest, comfort, healing, encouragement, grace, and forgiveness turned out to be the place where I wasn't wanted. I was damaged goods.

What amazed me most was the fact that it was the people in the "world" who never darkened the doorway of a church or gave consideration to the things of God who loved me and encouraged me! As a result, I quit attending worship, and I gave up on the Church. I didn't want anything to do with it. The pain and bitterness consumed me to the point that my heart became cold and hard. I no longer trusted anything or anyone. I hit rock bottom.

It was then that God began to work in my life to turn things around. God used a handful of people who loved me unconditionally to begin the healing and restoration that I needed so desperately. Each one of them was a Christian who knew the pain I was experiencing. These wonderful folks encouraged me to get back to attending worship. They knew I could only find healing through the Lord. Deep down, I knew they were right.

I finally gave in and attended a worship service for the first time in a while. I wish I could say I loved it and found it healing. Truthfully, I didn't want to be there or have any part of it. However, that's when I began to come to terms with how emotionally and spiritually sick I had become.

During that time, a longtime friend of mine, a retired pastor, reached out to me. At first our conversations were centered around how I was doing, how I was feeling, and how my children were doing. Eventually, our conversations dealt with the Lord and the ministry. It didn't take long for my friend to figure out I wanted nothing to do with ministry. Besides, who would want a divorced preacher?

One Wednesday evening I received a call from a deacon of a church that had just lost their pastor. Their pastor had resigned to lead another church. I didn't know this deacon or his church. He asked if I could fill in as pulpit supply until they found a pastor.

I told him that I was no longer preaching and then asked how he got my name and number. He told me that it wasn't important and kept insisting I come and preach at his church! I continued to refuse, but he told me to think and pray about it and that he would call back in a few days. After the call ended, I was angry. What part of "no" did he not understand?

I told my retired preacher friend about the call. That was when he unloaded on me. He told me that God was not finished with me and that it was time I got back to doing what God had called me to do! I told him that I had always been taught that if someone was divorced, they were disqualified from being a pastor. In response, he asked me three questions.

"Do you believe God is an all-knowing God?"

"Yes," I replied.

"Do you believe that when God called you into the ministry, He knew you would get divorced one day?"

Again, my response was "Yes."

"Do you believe the Bible?"
"Yes!"

He went on to quote Romans 11:29, "For the gifts and the callings of God are irrevocable." He ended the conversation by reminding me once again that it was time to get back to my calling.

The next day I phoned the deacon who had asked me to fill in at his church and told him that I would be there. I arrived at the church early that Sunday morning and met with the deacon to go over the service. All I had to do was to preach after I was introduced.

Terrified, I sat there waiting for my time to speak. I had not preached for some time, and it felt like I had never preached before in my life! I asked the Lord for strength, courage, and the words He would like me to say.

When I was introduced, I stepped up to the pulpit. As I opened my mouth, the words began to flow as if I had never been away from preaching. All I could do afterward was thank the Lord! He made it possible for me to be in ministry again from that day to the present. God has allowed me to pastor five churches since that day. The latest is a small church in southern Indiana. Praise the Lord!

I wish I could tell you that I'm completely healed of my brokenness, but I'm still a work in progress. There's no doubt that I'm much, much better than I was. But at times, bitterness still rears its head. Some days I have a hard time trusting, letting people love me, or showing love in return. I have even found myself shutting down and closing everyone out. But through it all, today I am a better pastor/preacher, husband, father, grandfather, and man. Like everyone, I have a ways to go, but thanks to the Lord and my wife, I'll get there!

Today, I am married to a beautiful, remarkable Christian woman. Not only is she my wife, she is also my best friend, my protector, and the love of my life. The Lord continues to use her in my healing. She is truly God sent. No one could ask for a better wife. I am truly blessed.

I'm so thankful for Jeff's honesty and willingness to share his story with you. Today there's an excitement in his walk with Christ like never before. It's clear that he loves his Lord, his wife, the Church, and its people. God is now using this broken man to love and help rebuild a local body of brokenhearted believers. The Holy Spirit is on the move and changing lives for God's glory in that little congregation, and Jeff is right in the center of it, leading the people. How do I know this? Brother Jeff is now my pastor.

6
Learning from the Eagles

> But those who wait upon the Lord shall renew their strength; They shall mount up with wings like eagles, They shall run and not be weary, They shall walk and not faint. (Is. 40:28–31, ESV)

One of the few birds God ever told us to be like is the eagle; pondering this has helped me more than once as

I've reflected on my life's journey. There's something intriguing about eagles. Their strength, beauty, and superiority are something to behold! When this magnificent creature soars through the air, it seems to be an effortless feat.

When possible, eagles build their nests in a tall tree or on a high cliff. They don't fly on their own energy but on the thermal currents of the wind. With their tremendous eyesight, eagles can see their prey while it is two to three miles away! Without making a sound, they fly toward their target at speeds up to 150 miles per hour and never lose their focus! Eagles are so strong that they can break a person's bones with their talons. Rarely would one think that this symbol of our great nation could ever be anything but strong. However, at least once in its life, this mighty bird goes through an extreme trauma called molting.

The molting process can bring about depression. Eagles begin to lose their feathers, and their beaks and claws will calcify. They begin to walk like turkeys, have no strength to fly, and are unable to hold their heads up. This is such a traumatic experience for this majestic bird that they lose their desire to eat. When possible, eagles eat fresh meat, but while molting they have no strength to hunt.

During this time, experts have observed other eagles coming and dropping food—fresh meat—to the ones going through this depression, heartache, and possible death. Yet, they've also noticed that it's never younger eagles that drop the food; it's always the older ones who have survived the experience and know what the molting eagle is going through. The survivors of molting also scream loudly, trying to encourage the molting birds below. Thankfully, some of the birds eat and recover, but others will not take the nourishment and merely roll over and die.

When it seems all hope is lost, another phenomenon takes place. As a molting eagle finds itself in this state, oftentimes it will choose an area of a mountain range where the sun can shine directly on it. The eagle will then lie on a rock, bathe in the sun, and allow its wings to heal.

Oh, how this speaks to me! There will come a time in every person's life when it seems as if everything is falling apart, and all hope is lost. But for born-again children of God, there's assurance!

Jesus said, "In the world you will have tribulation; but be of good cheer! I have overcome the world" (Jn. 16:33, NKJV).

Life isn't always lived soaring high above the mountains. We also experience dark valley experiences. Throughout my dark time, like the eagle, my desire for physical food diminished. I lost a lot of weight, quickly! Also, for a brief time, the same was true spiritually. Because I was at my lowest point, feeding on God's Word became an effort for which I had no desire. But that was exactly where I needed to be—in the Word! No wonder Peter tells us to "as newborn babes, desire the pure milk of the Word, so that you may grow thereby, if indeed you have tasted that the Lord is gracious" (1 Pet. 2:2–3, NKJV).

Just as eagles experience a loss of vision while molting, I suffered from the same problem. Because I was so broken, I couldn't see God's hand on me, but He was there—He always is! Sadly, sometimes even today, just for a moment, I still lose my vision. The storms come and rage around me, and all I see is the trial. I don't have enough vision to realize that my Savior is always with me in the storm. Because I'm His child, He's always leading me to a place of safety that only becomes clear to me when I keep Him in the center of my vision. It's also in those times that the sweet Holy Spirit reminds me that He's promised to never leave or forsake me (Num. 23:19; Heb. 13:5).

Molting also causes eagles to walk with their heads hanging down. Calcium builds up on their talons and beaks, much like hardness wraps itself around the human heart. During my time in the valley, it seemed as if God was far away and unresponsive. Therefore, I walked with my head and heart hanging so low while gradually allowing an unforgiving hardness to wrap around my soul.

Then, just as surely as other eagles gather to help and encourage molting eagles, fellow Christians are instructed by Paul's words in 1 Corinthians 1:3–4 to comfort those who are troubled with the comfort we ourselves have received from God. Looking back, I can see where some of my brothers and sisters in Christ have done that for me many times throughout my years of healing.

As eagles make their way to the sun for healing, the same principle applies to our lives. Healing will take place as we make our way to the Son and lay ourselves bare before Him to bathe in His presence while waiting for His touch.

Read Isaiah 40:31 once again: "But those who wait upon the Lord shall renew their strength; They shall mount up with wings like eagles, they shall run and not be weary, they shall walk and not faint."

"To wait," as in to wait on the Lord, is an intense verb in Hebrew. It means "to aggressively bind yourself to the Lord as you wait for Him to renew your strength."

7
Rebuilding His Temple

In 1 Kings 19 we see how God tenderly cared for Elijah after he came against the prophets of Baal on Mt. Carmel. Elijah had been on a spiritual high, but now he was afraid of Jezebel and Ahab. The stress of the moment set in when Elijah realized he had angered the king and queen and might be killed. So, he walked into the wilderness, lay down, and prayed to die. After falling asleep, he was awakened sometime later by an angel who said, "Arise and eat."

Elijah followed the instructions and then lay down again and slept. The angel woke him a second time and gave him food. Once again, Elijah followed the instructions. Then he continued in the strength of the Lord for forty days.

We are physical beings with physical needs. If we don't take proper care of ourselves, we get burned out, stressed out, tired, and sick. If we're not careful, we can compound mental anguish on top of the way we're feeling physically.

If you've ever suffered a serious illness, you know the road to recovery can be long. Regaining physical strength is a slow process, and you must take it one day at a time. The same rule applies when recovering from a spiritual setback. Yes, our relationship with Christ is restored the moment we ask for forgiveness and express our desire to have close fellowship with him again. He doesn't say, "Let's give it a few weeks and see how you do, and then I'll forgive and restore you to full fellowship." But when we've been severely hurt, our relationships with other people, our desire to minister, and different aspects of what our normal life was seem difficult to resume. We must step back and get our spiritual bearings before we are ready to proceed.

Throughout all my grief, worry, and feelings of total failure, a constant physical pain plagued me. I told my dad that I just wanted the pain to stop. In his usual wise and gentle way, he said, "It will stop. It won't be all at once, but over time it will get better."

Like a child, I pouted, saying, "I don't want it to stop over time. I want God to do it right now!" God, however, does not work on my timetable. In His time and in His way, the pain did stop, and healing came.

Looking back, I can clearly see how God was so faithful, gracious, and merciful. Without any conscious effort on my part, the Lord's healing and restoring hand was upon me. However, until some of the wounds began to heal, the constant pain in my stomach subsided, and the scars began to soften, I was unable to participate in the process. He alone is my true Healer.

As hard as it was, I also realized that as the mother of a second grader, I still had to deal with the realities of life. As bad as I wanted to withdraw from those around me—and life in general—I still had to get up in the morning and take care of my daughter. Even in my weak and broken state, she leaned on me for strength.

After my divorce, I told my mother that I would never sing again. Although the people in my church frequently asked me, I refused all invitations. While there was still no formal acknowledgment of my call to minister through the music, the Lord used these precious people with whom I worshiped each week to encourage me and to stir up God's gift within me (2 Tim. 1:6). Encouraging those who are broken is so important to the healing process!

My healing continued, and day by day, I began to draw closer to the Lord through Bible reading and prayer. My mother gave me a new Bible, and it quickly became an instrument of the Lord in my hands. I began to desire the milk of the Word and grow by it. I had tasted and seen that the Lord was full of grace (1Pet. 2:2–3). The more time I spent in the Word, the more I felt His strength overcoming my weakness. My new Bible became a cherished friend, and though it is worn and tattered now, it is a reminder of all that the Lord has brought me through. He reminds me daily of His promise that He will never leave me (Heb.13:5b).

As the Lord continued the restoration process, my self-worth, trust, confidence, and sense of humor began to return. When I reflected on all that had taken place and the work of healing that God was doing in me, my life began to take an upward turn. I could feel myself beginning to move forward as I saw the effects of God's hand in my life once again.

The summer after my divorce, I won a vocal contest in Pipestem, West Virginia. It gave me the confidence to continue with my music, although only occasionally at church and in nursing home services.

The Lord then sent a wonderful man into my life who did for me what Boaz did for Ruth, rescuing me in almost the same way. Greg Taylor rented a house from my father and moved in just down the road from us. He and I met at the local grocery store one evening quite by accident. You never can tell what may happen when two people run into each other in the produce department! Several days later he showed up at my parents' house and visited for a few minutes with them and me. Later, he admitted that he was simply "checking out the territory." Our first date was two weeks after that, and it was obvious that the Lord had been at work on my behalf! Greg and I got married three and a half months later. As of this writing, that was thirty-four years ago!

Within three years the Lord blessed us with a son, Philip. Life without my daughter, son, and husband would be unimaginable!

When I speak about Greg as my rescuer, it's more than the fact that he came along when I felt like a stranger in a foreign land. It is also more than the fact that his family accepted my daughter and me as if we had always been a part of them. You see, my legal name is Cheryl Ruth (please don't call me that), and my mother-in-law's name is Naomi. Coincidence? I don't think so. All of this and so much more reminds me that I serve a God of second chances.

Greg & Cheri Taylor

Cheri & Heather

Cheri & Philip

8
Restoration Through Repentance

As I stated in an earlier chapter, I've often seen how others perceive divorced people differently, especially in the Church. I've seen the looks of some toward the broken as if they are now "less than." I've also heard words spoken in condemnation while pointing fingers and heaping more shame upon shattered lives. Before my divorce, I must admit that I did the same.

Isn't it amazing how we who claim the

name of Christ sometimes put ourselves on these little white pedestals proclaiming judgment on those around us? Yet, if the truth be told, most of us have sins hidden away that would cause each of us tremendous shame if anyone found out. God have mercy!

This reminds me of the woman caught in adultery in John 8:1–11. The religious leaders of the day, the scribes and Pharisees, brought her to Jesus, ready to condemn her and stone her! Yet, the words Jesus spoke still ring in my heart: "He who is without sin among you, let him throw a stone at her first" (John 8:7, NKJV). One by one, they turned and left.

Please hear my heart: sin must be dealt with! Many of the world's problems today arise from the fact that we have turned our backs on true biblical teaching while making the vile and evil acceptable! God is not pleased with this, and we will be judged! Remember, this book is speaking about people who are broken, like me, who need restoration and love.

Many years ago, I was preparing to sing with a group for an event. Before things started, one of the leaders pulled me aside and said I was never to acknowledge my divorce. Once again, I felt like one of those who was considered "less than." I was already embarrassed by my failure and my situation, but his words pushed me down even further.

I also remember the story of a friend who got divorced several years before I was. Now serving the Lord, he was also a gospel singer, like me. One Sunday, the group he traveled with was scheduled to sing in his home church. However, he was not allowed to stand on the main platform with the rest of the quartet while they sang. Because of his divorce, he was forced to stand on the second step during the service! When I first heard the story, I must admit, I laughed! Now it isn't funny; it's sad.

Many people believe that divorce is an unforgivable sin. Some believe that once a Christian divorces, God no longer has any use for them. What's in their minds that makes divorce so unpardonable? Does God forgive lying? Yes. Does He forgive murder? Yes.

Does He forgive divorce? Yes. The requirement for obtaining forgiveness for all sin is the same: confession of our sins to God and asking for forgiveness (1 Jn. 1:9).

Many people believe there are other sins that fall into the category of rendering us useless in God's service. I have some close friends who, before they came to know Christ, had an abortion. After they came to Christ for forgiveness and restoration, God was able to use their past to help bring many to His throne for forgiveness and freedom. This is not to say that "big sins" enable us to minister more effectively; it's just pointing out that God can use us despite big sins and in spite of ourselves!

Second Corinthians 1:3–4 tells us that we have a responsibility to tell, to comfort, and to let others have the benefit of knowing that what God has done for us, He can do for them!

9
God's Strength Is Sufficient

Even after my divorce, my idea of success was worldly. I still didn't get it. What does God have to do in our lives, and in our children's lives, to get us to the place where He can use us? When do we become willing to do whatever it takes to become what He wants us to be?

To get to the place God could use me, I had to allow Him to rearrange my priorities. I had to get the stars out of my eyes, so I could see the path He had set for me.

I had to let Him give a new definition of the word "success." Discovering that success did not mean having a huge radio hit, a number-one song on the Top 40 chart, or becoming a household name across the nation was a rude awakening for me.

God showed me that there were things that He had for me that would bring unspeakable joy, even if no one ever heard me sing a note. Romans 12:1–2 exhorts us to become living sacrifices and present ourselves to God. Then the Word cautions us not to conform ourselves to the world but to be transformed by renewing our minds, so we can prove what the good, acceptable, and perfect will of God is. In following the instructions given here, we find true success—not as the world gives but as God gives. And what God gives to us, the world can never take away.

As my confidence in my calling grew, so did my desire to expand and go to more places. I would lay prostrate on my floor, begging God to open doors of opportunity. However, He knows our future and all that it holds. Ecclesiastes 3:1 (KJV) says, "To everything there is a season, a time for every purpose under Heaven," even our irrevocable callings.

Finally, my ministry started to move in a positive direction, and I was excited! I had recorded several projects and released a number of radio singles. My network of people in the music industry also started to look impressive. My first producer was well connected to the Gaither ministry, and my current producer is highly sought after. He's also a nationally known Gospel Music radio personality! Bookings were up, and churches were calling me to come and sing. Life was good, and I was really making progress. I felt that I was well on my way to being healed and restored. Then, suddenly, the bottom fell out.

I've heard it said that many pastors "quit" every Monday morning. They pour themselves out Sunday after Sunday, seemingly to no avail. No one in the congregation seems to be moved by what

God has said through them, and discouragement sets in. Others in ministry often face the same obstacles.

On one occasion I was having a hard time booking dates. Churches and promoters alike were saying, "Sorry, we don't have any open dates for you right now." Praying and crying out to the Lord yielded no results, and discouragement set in. I was ready to quit, and I said so to my husband in no uncertain terms. Greg looked at me for a moment. "No, you are not ready to quit," he said. Then he suggested I call a longtime mentor of mine, Brother Walter.

As I sat before this trusted friend, I poured out my heart. He listened quietly as I told him about the progress I had made with my singing career and how things had been going so well. Then I said, "Suddenly, I can't get bookings to go sing! I feel as if I have nothing else to give!" I continued to express my frustration, discouragement, hurt feelings, and burnout, stating that I was ready to quit.

After I finished my pity party, this kind, gentle, and honest man looked me in the eye and said, "Well, good! Now God can do something with you!"

Looking back at that moment, I realize how self-sufficiency had taken hold of me. As long as I was working in my own strength, God could not manifest His strength in me. The Apostle Paul puts it this way:

> Because of the extravagance of those revelations, and so I wouldn't get a big head, I was given the gift of a handicap to keep me in constant touch with my limitations. Satan's angel did his best to get me down; what he in fact did was push me to my knees. No danger then of walking around high and mighty. At first, I didn't think of it as a gift, and begged God to re-

move it. Three times I did that, and then He told me, "My grace is enough; it's all you need. My strength comes into its own in your weakness." Once I heard that, I was glad to let it happen. I quit focusing on the handicap and began appreciating the gift. It was a case of Christ's strength moving in on my weakness. Now I take limitations in stride, and with good cheer, these limitations that cut me down to size—abuse, accidents, opposition, bad breaks. I just let Christ take over! And so, the weaker I get, the stronger I become. (2 Cor. 12:7–10, *The Message*)

Problems with arranging the priorities in my life manifested themselves through my attempt at being self-sufficient. I wanted to "do" while God wanted me to "be." We can never do enough to put ourselves into a right standing with God. Only through God's gifts of mercy and grace can we be in a proper relationship with Him and be all that He wants us to be for His glory.

A simplified definition of "unmerited favor" means that God gives us what we do not deserve. When we trust Jesus as our Savior, God forgives our sins, takes the blood of Jesus shed on the cross as payment for our sins, and brings us into His family.

Mercy, on the other hand, means that God does not give us what we deserve. Because of His holiness, God cannot even look upon sin. Our sin makes us worthy of just one thing—death. But in God's mercy, He does not require that payment from us. Instead, He takes the death of Jesus and applies it to our account.

So, because of mercy and grace, we can be in relationship with God as He intended us to be from the beginning of creation.

I began to realize that my desire to sing or minister in some other way was prompted by a tendency most of us have at some point in our lives, the part of us that says, "I do a lot for God!" How arrogant we are! My parents taught me by word and by example that the first priority in life is to follow the instruction in Matthew 6:33: "Seek ye first the kingdom of God and His righteousness." This is the "be" part. If we do this, we will be in a right relationship with God. It will also place us into a right relationship with other people, and then we will be well on our way to becoming the people whom God intended us to be.

Once I got the "be" part of the equation, God added the "do." When my schedule is empty, instead of begging God to help me fill it, I ask Him what He is trying to show me or teach me. This causes me to grow closer to Him.

10
His Healing Power

There are so many other things that God has done for me through the last four decades. I firmly believe that all of them were for my good. I have had to make a conscious effort to remind myself that when strong winds want to sink my ship and take me under, there is no need to be afraid. As Joel Hemphill wrote so beautifully, "I know the Master of the Wind." Because I do know Him, I can be confident that even when I can't see exactly what God is doing, I can trust Him to always do what is best for me.

There is a condition to knowing for sure that everything is working out for our good. Romans 8:28 (KJV) tells us, "And we know that all things work together for good to them that love God, to them who are called according to His purpose." We must love God and be called according to His purpose. We must know Jesus as our personal Savior.

With that thought in mind, I must ask you to make sure that you do know Him. You cannot begin to hope for God's healing and restoration in your life if you are not His child. Many believe that we are all God's children. This is not true. While we are all God's creation, only those who receive Jesus as their Lord and Savior become the children of God. "But as many as received Him, to them He gave the power [authority] to become children of God, to those who believe in His name" (Jn. 1:12, KJV).

If I did not have assurance of my salvation experience, I would never have had the strength to deal with the fact that my life had been shattered. My parents were there to help in any possible way, but they could not heal me. Only having the "peace of God that passes all understanding" that Paul talks about in Philippians 4:7 gave me the courage to face what I needed to do. God gives the same peace to all of His children.

If you are not sure that you have been born again, that you have a personal relationship with Jesus, I urge you to make Him a reality in your life. It will be the most important decision you ever make.

When I speak at women's events, I have the privilege of meeting and counseling with many individuals who have walked the same bitter path and come to believe that God cannot—or will not—use them.

They look around at the couples and the families in their churches and think, *I wish that could be me. I wish God would just speak to my heart and tell me He loves me and that He wants me to be a part of His work.* Then they confess to me that what I have said is fine for me, but it has no application in their lives. They cannot seem to grasp the fact that they've allowed the past to hold them in bondage.

In Luke 4:18, Jesus quotes Isaiah 61:1 when He says, "The Spirit of the Lord is upon me, because He hath anointed me to preach the gospel to the poor; He hath sent me to heal the broken-hearted, to preach deliverance to the captives." He followed this up with, "This day is this scripture fulfilled in your ears" (KJV).

This is what Jesus has given me to share with those of you whom Satan is holding in bondage to your past. If you have made ashes of your life, Jesus will trade those ashes for beauty. If you are in mourning, He will give you the oil of joy in exchange. Jesus will trade your spirit of heaviness for the garment of praise, and He will do all of this to bring glory to His Father.

This is why I can tell you with full assurance that Jesus will do for you everything He has done for me! He will forgive and heal you. No matter the source of your shame—divorce, poverty, abuse, abandonment, spiritual neglect, abortion, alternative lifestyles, or anything else—God will take it and make your life brand new. If you have been healthy and whole spiritually before, He will restore you. If you have never been in good spiritual health, God will take you there. There is nothing He will not do for the good of those who love Him.

On the Other Side

Restoration of the heart along with a sense of calm and well-being were probably the last steps in healing my brokenness. The enemy, however, was not willing to let me experience this last step without a fight.

A few years ago, I was falsely accused of spreading lies about someone. In my innocence, I cried out to the Lord, "Why would they do this? I don't understand! Lord, I need to hear from You now!" I picked up my Bible, and it fell open to 2 Corinthians 1:3–4 (KJV): "Blessed be the God and Father of our Lord Jesus Christ, the Father of mercies and the God of all comfort, who comforts us in all our tribulations, that we may be able to comfort those who are in any trouble, with the comfort with which we ourselves are comforted by God." I still didn't understand it all, but I knew that the Lord had a purpose.

Today, much of the ministry I've been called to revolves around this passage. I'm still amazed at how God brings across my path, people who have gone through, or are going through, the same thing I experienced. Now I can say to them with a calm assurance, "Let me tell you what my Lord has done for me!"

The path to restoration begins at the cross. It does not lie within us, our friends, our families, or any other human. The path lies completely in Christ Jesus. In Him only will you find the healing and restoration you seek.

This path is a process; there is no quick fix. Staying in the Word and on your knees is vital to this process. Sometimes we get off the path, but when we do, Jesus waits patiently for us to return to Him.

Jeff Ferguson wrote a song titled "There You Are" that expresses my feelings exactly about God's restoration. Just when I thought there was no way I could ever enjoy fellowship with Him again, and just when I thought I had done more than God could forgive, I looked up, and He was waiting for me with open arms. The following lines from that song are especially meaningful to me.

> There You are,
> Faithfully pouring out mercy,
> Mending my heart
> Just when I thought I'd wandered too far,
> There You are.

I understand that my sin has consequences that not even God's forgiveness can remove. But my past does not determine the future that the Lord has for me, and neither does yours. He takes us just as we are—in our sin and brokenness—and He helps us realize that He is the only One who can forgive, heal, and restore. But He can only do this when we give Him full control of our lives and submit to His will. Then He will move us past the dark, lonely, fearsome place to "the other side of broken."

Cheri with Les Butler "Back in the Day"

Cheri and Les, still serving the Lord with gladness after 20 years

Cheri with her dear friend, Aaron Wilburn (1950-2020)

Notes

Amy Morris, Dave Clark, and Marty Hennis. 1995. "The Other Side of Broken." Track 3 on *I'm a Believer*. Myrrh Records, CD.

Jeff Ferguson and Reba Rambo. 2008. "There You Are." Track 10 on *Do It*. Muzik Group, CD.

DBA Music of Evergreen
A/C Jeff Ferguson Music
PO Box 24149
Nashville, TN 37202

Belden Street Music Publishing
C/o Songs of Evergreen Copyrights
C/o Evergreen Copyrights Inc.
PO Box 24149
Nashville, TN 37202

Experience Worship Music Publishing
C/o Songs of Evergreen Copyrights
C/o Evergreen Copyrights
PO Box 24149
Nashville, TN. 37202

Rambo McGuire Music
PO Box 50508
Nashville, TN 37205

About the Author

Following the path that God has placed before her for nearly forty-five years, Cheri Taylor is blessed with a dynamic singing voice, an exciting stage presence. She delights in being a Gospel Music powerhouse at concerts and special events while presenting God's Word to her audiences. Serving now as a solo performer, recording artist, radio personality, and speaker for women's events, Cheri travels extensively throughout the United States, hosting live events.

Since 1998, Cheri has recorded numerous albums while receiving recognition through various awards. She is a former member of the Conference of Southern Baptist Evangelists and has been endorsed by the North American Mission Board.

Her husband, Greg, works alongside her at home and on the road in every phase of Cheri Taylor Ministries. "Greg has been so supportive of me," Cheri says. "Even through times of discouragement, he has been there, cheering me on." When Cheri is not engaged in her personal ministry efforts, she serves in the body of her local church and works with a ministry that serves the citizens of Jamaica.

Cheri and Greg have two grown and married children, Heather and Philip, along with four fabulous grandchildren. Heather and her husband, Andy, are parents to Ryan and Ryker. Heather is the owner and lead teacher of Dance Haven Studios in southern Indiana. Andy, who served as a rescue swimmer in the United States Navy, is now a boat captain for Mulzer Crushed Stone. Philip and his wife, Jamie, also have two children, Amelia and Abraham (a.k.a., Abe) and reside in southern Indiana. Philip served as a United States Marine in Afghanistan and Japan and now works for Miller Pipeline as a machine operator. Jamie is a homeschooling mom, chicken farmer, and multi-talented lady.

Experience Cheri's latest Album, *Comin' Out Singin'*, now available for purchase or download.

Interested in booking Cheri for your next women's conference or retreat? We'd love to hear from you!

Cheri Taylor Ministries
PO Box 22
Santa Claus, IN 47579
Call: (812) 549-8199
Email: cheritaylor@psci.net
www.CheriTaylor.org

www.ingramcontent.com/pod-product-compliance
Lightning Source LLC
Chambersburg PA
CBHW072012290426
44109CB00018B/2218